W9-BFG-736

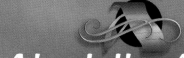

About the Author™

Meet

Patricia MacLachlan

Frances E. Ruffin

The Rosen Publishing Group's
PowerKids Press™
New York

For Marise and Melvin Smith

Published in 2006 by The Rosen Publishing Group, Inc.
29 East 21st Street, New York, NY 10010

First Edition

Editor: Rachel O'Connor
Layout Design: Julio A. Gil
Photo Researcher: Cindy Reiman

Photo Credits: Cover Photo by John MacLachlan, provided by HarperCollins Publishers; pp. 4, 5, 8, 11, 22 Courtesy of Patricia MacLachlan; p. 6 © Bettmann/Corbis; p. 7 © Tom & Dee Ann McCarthy/Corbis; p. 9 Courtesy of Archives & Special Collections at the Thomas J. Dodd Research Center, University of Connecticut; p. 12 Courtesy of Children's Aid and Family Service, Northampton, Massachusetts; p. 15 Nicole DiMella; p. 19 © Michael Lewis/National Geographic/Getty Images; p. 20 Judy Messer.

Grateful acknowlegement is made for permission to reprint previously published material:
p. 10 From BABY by Patricia MacLachlan. Published by Random House, Inc.
p. 14 From ARTHUR FOR THE VERY FIRST TIME by Patricia MacLachlan. Text copyright © 1980 by Patricia MacLachlan. Used by permission of HarperCollins Publishers.
p. 16 From SARAH, PLAIN AND TALL by Patricia MacLachlan. Jacket art copyright © 1985 by Marcia Sewall. Used by permission of HarperCollins Publishers.
p. 17 From SARAH, PLAIN AND TALL by Patricia MacLachlan. Copyright © 1985 by Patricia MacLachlan. Used by permission of HarperCollins Publishers.
p. 18 From JOURNEY by Patricia MacLachlan. Published by Random House, Inc.

Library of Congress Cataloging-in-Publication Data

Ruffin, Frances E.
    Meet Patricia MacLachlan / Frances E. Ruffin.— 1st ed.
        p. cm. — (About the author)
    Includes index.
    ISBN 1-4042-3130-7 (lib. bdg.)
    1. MacLachlan, Patricia—Juvenile literature. 2. Authors, American—20th century—Biography—Juvenile literature. 3. Children's stories—Authorship—Juvenile literature. I. Title. II. Series.
    PS3563.A3178Z85 2006
    813'.54—dc22

2004028238

Manufactured in the United States of America

Contents

Here is Patricia when she was five years old. As a child, Patricia read many books. By the time she was eight, however, she had already decided she would never try to become a writer. She believed that writers had all the answers and that she did not.

Find Out Who You Are

When Patricia MacLachlan was a little girl, her mother told her to "read a book and find out who you are." The fact that she and her parents lived in a house full of books helped her discover how much she loved writing.

Patricia's first **published** book was *The Sick Day*. It is a story about a day when Patricia's husband and her daughter stayed home with the flu. Patricia was 41 when she wrote the book. Many writers begin their **careers** when they are much younger. Even her daughter, Emily, thought her mother was "pretty old." However, her late start has never bothered her young readers.

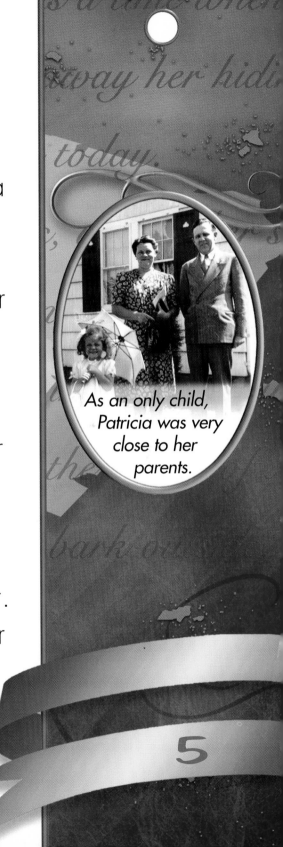

As an only child, Patricia was very close to her parents.

5

Imaginary Friends

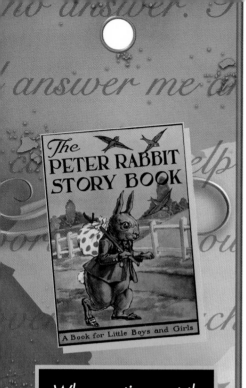

The PETER RABBIT STORY BOOK
A Book for Little Boys and Girls

When acting out the parts in Peter Rabbit, *Patricia would play Mr. MacGregor and her father would play Peter Rabbit. Then they would switch.*

Patricia was born on March 3, 1938, in Cheyenne, Wyoming. She was the only child of Philo and Madonna Moss Pritzkau, who were both teachers. Patricia was a happy child with an active **imagination**. She loved to make up imaginary people, and she created stories about them. She invented a friend named Mary and also made up a mother for Mary. Even Patricia's parents accepted Mary and her mother as part of the household. When she was very young, Patricia and her father enjoyed acting out scenes from her favorite books. They often changed the **plots** and the endings. Some days they would act out stories such as Peter Rabbit more than 25 times.

Children often dress up and pretend to be someone else, like the girls shown here. According to Patricia acting out stories can help people prepare for the things that might happen to them in their lives.

Patricia met her husband, Robert, at the University of Connecticut. Robert was studying to become a clinical psychologist, or someone who helps troubled people. Here they are on their wedding day on April 14, 1962.

A Move East

In 1944, when Patricia was six, the family moved to Rochester, Minnesota, where her father became director of that city's school system. Four years later they moved again, to Storrs, Connecticut.

Patricia **graduated** from high school in 1956. That fall she went to the University of Connecticut, where she majored in English. Hoping to learn some new skills, Patricia left college two years later. She found an office job with Prentice Hall, a large publishing company in New Jersey. Her job allowed Patricia to **mature** and to better **appreciate** her studies. She returned to college and graduated in 1962. That year she married her boyfriend, Robert MacLachlan.

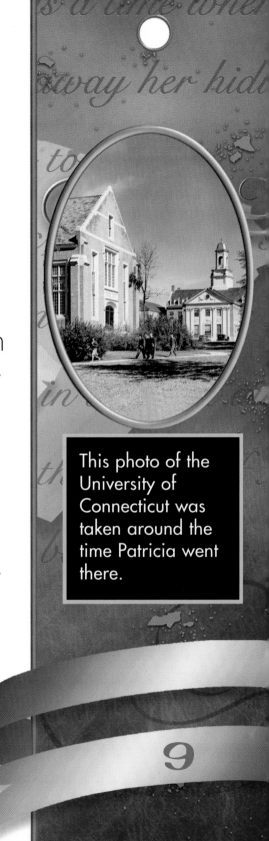

This photo of the University of Connecticut was taken around the time Patricia went there.

Starting a Family

In the fall of 1962, Patricia taught English to middle-school students in Manchester, Connecticut. She had a hard year as a new teacher. Her classes were large, and she was **inexperienced**. Patricia was happy when she and Robert moved to Bridgeport, Connecticut.

After the move Patricia gave up teaching, and the couple began a family. They had two sons and a daughter. During free moments in her life as a wife and a mother, Patricia spent time observing other people. She wrote her thoughts about what she saw in a **journal**. Writing in her journal about what she saw and what she thought led to her career in writing.

Patricia loved to spend time reading to her young children. Here she reads to her sons, John (standing) and Jamie.

Here you can see the entrance to the Children's Aid and Family Service in Northampton, Massachusetts.

Starting to Write

Patricia made another move with her husband and children, this time to Northampton, Massachusetts. With all her children in school, Patricia now had more time on her hands. She got **involved** with the Children's Aid and Family Service, where she served on the board from 1970 to 1980. The agency helped families and children who were in trouble and needed help.

Patricia also found time to take a course in writing for children. Jane Yolen, a well-known author, taught the class. Ms. Yolen sent one of Patricia's stories to an **agent**. The agent in turn sent it to the publishing house Harper & Row. Harper bought the book, which was later called *Through Grandpa's Eyes*.

Patricia began observing people as a child. She liked to listen to adults talk while she hid under the dining-room table, which was covered by a huge tablecloth. In 1982, she wrote *Cassie Binegar*, a book about a girl who listens to what people are saying while she hides. After reading the book, Patricia's mother sent her the dining-room tablecloth from their house.

Writing from Life

> "They ate Moira's goosh pie, which was really beef stew in bowls that tilted sideways on the slanted kitchen table. Moira's braces slipped, and they laughed into their mugs of milk."
>
> —From p. 43, Arthur, For the Very First Time

A **biographer** who wrote about Patricia's life says that, more than most authors, Patricia MacLachlan writes about the people she has known and about the events in her own life. In her book *Mama One, Mama Two*, she wrote a story about a little girl who lives with a **foster** mother while her mother is sick. Patricia based the book on the real-life stories of the children she knew while working with the Children's Aid and Family Service.

In 1980, Patricia wrote her first **novel** for older children, *Arthur, For the Very First Time*. It won an American Library Association Notable Book **Award** and the Golden Kite Award for **fiction**.

In Arthur, For the Very First Time, an only child, Arthur Rasby, changes his bad behavior after spending a summer in the country with a great-aunt and great-uncle.

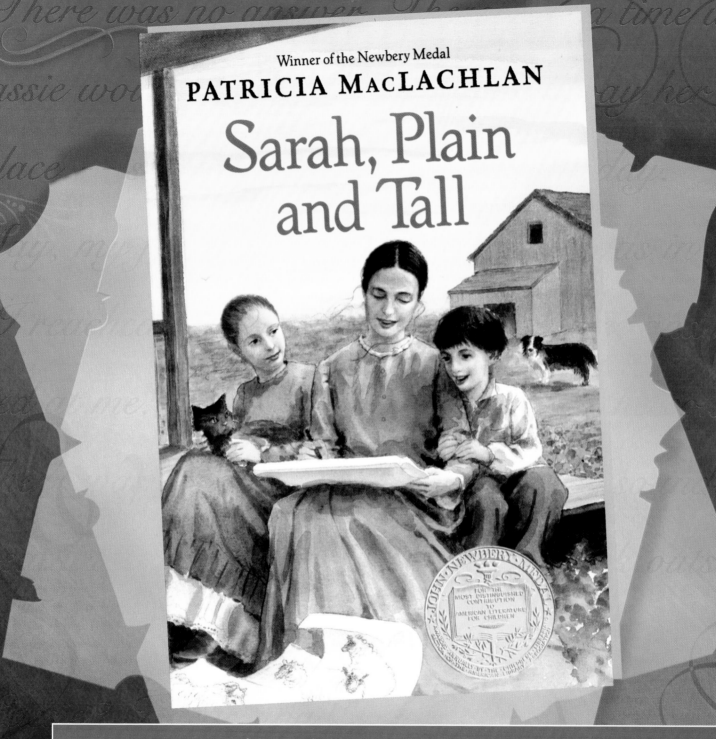

WINNER OF THE NEWBERY MEDAL

PATRICIA MacLACHLAN

Sarah, Plain and Tall

Patricia was very proud to win the Newbery Medal for Sarah, Plain and Tall, especially since it was a book that told part of her family's history.

Sarah, Plain and Tall

Patricia had been thinking about the story *Sarah, Plain and Tall* for many years before she wrote the book. Published in 1985, it is about a woman from Maine who answers an ad for a **mail-order bride**. A **widower** who lives on a midwestern **prairie** places the ad. His wife died and he needed a wife and mother for his two children. Years before Patricia's mother told her about the real family member on whom the book *Sarah, Plain and Tall* was based. Like the Sarah in the book, Sarah had answered an ad for a wife. She traveled west to marry Patricia's great-grandfather. In 1986, *Sarah* won the Newbery Medal. This is America's most important award for children's **literature**.

> *"The sheep made Sarah smile. She sank her fingers into their thick coarse wool. She talked to them, running with the lambs, letting them suck on her fingers. She named them after her favorite aunts, Harriet and Mattie and Lou."*
>
> —From p. 41, Sarah, Plain and Tall

What You Know First

In Patricia's book *What You Know First*, a young girl and her family prepare to leave their prairie farm to move to a new home near the ocean. The girl walks around the farm to take one last look at the things and places she wants to remember. The girl wants to carry the memories of her old home with her because it was the place she knew first.

Patricia often talks with her young readers about a place in their lives that most holds their memories. It is often a place where they felt comfortable and safe. Whenever she travels Patricia always carries a bag of prairie dirt with her. It reminds her of her childhood in Cheyenne, Wyoming, the place she knew first.

"... I sat for a long time, staring at Mama's picture, as if I could will her to turn and talk to the person next to her. If I looked at the picture long enough, my mama would move, stretch, smile at my grandfather behind the camera. But she didn't. I turned away, but her face stayed with me. The expression on Mama's face was one I knew. One I remembered."

—From p. 12, Journey

Pictured here is a hayfield in Cheyenne, Wyoming. Patricia lived in Cheyenne until her family moved to Minnesota when she was six years old.

This family photo was taken in 2003. From left to right are Patricia's son John, her daughter, Emily, her son Jamie, Patricia, and her husband, Bob. Patricia's father, Philo Pritzkau, who is seated, died the year after the photograph was taken. He was 102.

At Home

Today Patricia and Robert live near the Massachusetts home where they raised their children. Their children are now adults. Patricia's oldest son, John, works in Africa, and her son Jamie works in publishing. Patricia has written three books with her daughter, Emily, who works with children. "When we write stories together, I can't tell her words from mine," Patricia says. When she is not writing, Patricia reads and spends time with her dogs, Charlie and Emmet. She and Robert also enjoy playing music. She plays the cello and he plays the viola. When traveling Patricia always brings at least eight books with her. In case of an **accident**, she will have something to read while waiting to be saved!

Patricia's workday does not fit a set pattern. All her writing days are different. Sometimes she works early and all through the day. Those are the days that her writing is going well. Other days she finds it hard to write. On such days she takes her dogs for walks or plays solitaire on her computer!

In Her Own Words

Patricia says she does not write because it is easy. She writes because it is hard.

When did you know you wanted to be a writer?
I have always known I wanted to be a writer, even when I was a child. Books have always been the most important things in my life, other than my family and dogs. They have always been like old friends that were there for you forever.

Why did you decide to write for children?
I like writing for children because I like and respect children. But also, if a children's book is good it is good for adults as well. That way I have a large audience.

What do you enjoy best about your job?
I love it when a character says something that surprises me, or when I write a paragraph that I like. Mostly I like what I do because I can change life and make it come out the way I want it to. Most times, that is. Some days my characters lead me to new places.

What would you like readers to take away from your books?
I think I want my readers to find themselves in my books. Or perhaps recognize that I have some of the same worries and concerns that they do. I want to reach out and touch my reader.

If you weren't a writer, what would you be doing instead?
If I weren't a writer I might like to be a painter. I love color and form. I guess that is really what I try to do by writing. I am trying to paint a picture.

Glossary

accident (AK-seh-dent) An unexpected and sometimes bad event.

agent (AY-jent) A person who helps a writer, actor, or sports player with his or her job.

appreciate (uh-PREE-shee-ayt) To understand the value of.

award (uh-WORD) Something that is given after careful thought.

biographer (by-AH-gruh-fur) Someone who writes books that give a history of people's lives.

careers (kuh-REERZ) Jobs.

fiction (FIK-shun) Stories that tell about people and events that are not real.

foster (FOS-tur) Not related by birth or adoption.

graduated (GRAH-joo-wayt-ed) To have finished a course of school.

imagination (ih-ma-jih-NAY-shun) Being able to create things in your mind.

inexperienced (in-ek-SPEER-ee-unst) New at something.

involved (in-VOLVD) Kept busy by something.

journal (JER-nul) A notebook in which people write their thoughts.

literature (LIH-tuh-ruh-chur) Writings such as books, plays, and poetry.

mail-order bride (MAYL-or-dur BRYD) A woman who answers an ad to get married.

mature (muh-TOOR) To become full-grown.

novel (NAH-vul) A long story about made-up people and events.

plots (PLOTS) The events that happen in a story.

prairie (PRER-ee) A large area of flat land with grass but few or no trees.

published (PUH-blishd) Printed so that people can read it.

widower (WIH-deh-wer) A man whose wife has died.

Index

Web Sites

Due to the changing nature of Internet links, PowerKids Press has developed an online list of Web sites related to the subject of this book. This site is updated regularly. Please use this link to access the list: www.powerkidslinks.com/aa/patmaclac/